THE GATHERING YEARS
A SMALL TEENAGE GUIDE

Author
Sharvesh Sivakumar

Publisher:
Viveka Pathippagam
Vazhapadi, Salem-636115.

First published in **2025**
First edition
Author: **Sharvesh Sivakumar**
Pages: **84**
Font Point: 12
Rate: Rs.**100**
Published by:
Viveka Pathippagam, Vazhapadi,
Salem dt. TamilNadu- 636115.
vivekapathippagam@gmail.com

ABOUT THE AUTHOR

DREAMS AND DESIRES WE LIVE TODAY....

I am Sharvesh Sivakumar a 14-year-old teenager and a school studying boy, a person who has the passion for writing and story telling always love books and I believe magic happens in reading a book. I was just in class 8 when I wrote this book.

I have always loved reading and have completed 30 books in the past two years, making me a book worm. Until 2024, I was just like any other kid-I went to school, did my homework, scrolled through YouTube, ate, and slept without much worries about anything else.

But last year, something changed. I started focusing on my academics, personal growth, mental well-being, and physical health. I wanted to improve myself and be more mindful of my life. In 2025, I took it a step further and started caring about my appearance, paying attention to how I looked and presented myself.

It's been a journey of self-improvement, and I feel like I'm on the right path. As it was rightly said,

"The only person you are destined to become is the person you decide to be "- Ralph Waldo Emerson

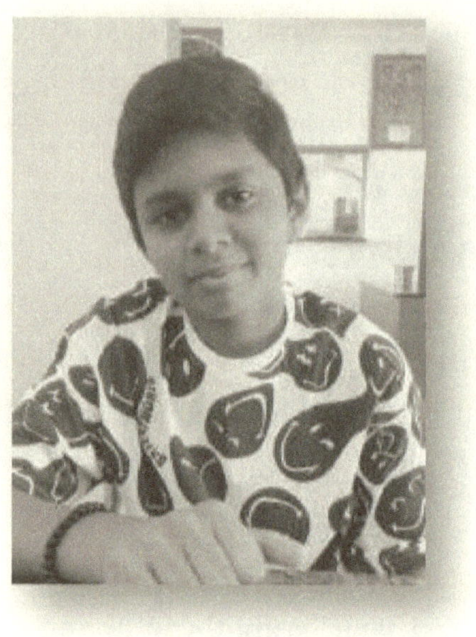

-Sharvesh Sivakumar

UNFOLDING MY STORY

This book is a reflection of everything I have realized about my life, school, exams, and productivity. It is a collection of lessons learned, mistakes made, and strategies that helped me improve.

I wrote this book for teenagers like me-those who care about their future and want to do better in school, manage time wisely, build confidence, and improve themselves. Being a teenager isn't easy.

We juggle academics, friendships, and personal growth, yet no one teaches us how to balance it all. That's why I wanted to share what I've learned-to help others navigate their journey more effectively.

This book is not just about school; it's about becoming the best version of you-academically, mentally, and physically. You'll learn how to study smarter, stay productive, beat procrastination, and take control of your life.

Self-improvement is a journey, and small, consistent efforts lead to big changes. If you've ever felt like you could be doing more but didn't know where to start, this book is for you. Let's begin this journey together.

Publisher's view..

I am Dr.P.Periyar Mannan, I am founder of Viveka Publications in Vazhappadi, Salem district. I have written and published many books, including songs, stories and short stories that teach moral values to school children. My songs have been included in the Sahitya Akademi's children's songs collection book.

Selvan. Sharvesh Sivakumar is son of KVS. Sivakumar – M.Savitha lives in Salem Tamilnadu. He is a student studying in class IX at the nearby School.

He met me with his parent and our family friend Thiruveni earth movers company CEO Mr C.Kumaresan at the end of May 2025. He gave me a manuscript it is his written for develop self-confidence to teenagers. he asked me to publish them as a book titled **The Gathering years** '.

Realy I was stunned when I read this book. I was amazed that this student, this book is not only teenage school children, but also people of all ages can enrich their minds and qualities. I have read this book in its entirety as an publisher and it is truly a wonderful book. My congratulations and appreciation to the author Sharvesh Sivakumar. He is sure to emerge as one of the best English language writers in Tamil Nadu in the future. I urge everyone, including students and teachers, to buy and read this book.

Thank you.

Dr.P.PeriyarMannan Ph.D.,
Viveka Publications,
Vazhapadi,Salem(Dt).

BOOK OUTLINE

PART 1: LIFE

- WHEN YOU START THE DAY EARLY
- THE 30 MINUTE WORKOUT THAT CHANGES THE LIFE
- YOUR EMOTION AND MOOD SWINGS
- SMALL THINGS THAT GIVE VERY BIG RESULTS
- THE ARCHIVE OF THE LIFE

PART 2: PRODUCTIVITY

- WHY DO STUFF WE DO ARE SO MORE AT LAST
- THE SMALL KNOWLEDGE GAINING LETTERS
- THE TIMER THAT SAVER THE TIME
- HOW TO COMPLETE 30 BOOKS PER YEAR EVEN WHEN YOU GO TO SCHOOL
- THE HABIT OF WRITING BOOK

PART 3: SCHOOL

- HOW I GET MARKS IN MY EXAM

- ➢ OUR MOST TRUSTABLE (BUT NOT) ONES
- ➢ THE EXTRA TIME YOU WASTE A LOT
- ➢ WHAT STUDIYING ACTUALLY MEAN
- ➢ THE ONE TECHNIQUE THAT MADE ME A GOOD LEARNER

THE PLAN FOR FURTHER USE LETS TRY TOGETHER.- ACTION PLAN

How to get the most out of the book!

If this isn't your first book, feel free to use whatever method works best for you. Make the book yours. However, if this is your first time reading a book with the intention of learning and applying what you read, I'd like to share some tips to help you make the most of it.

1. Tools you'll need

To actively engage with this book (or any book you read for learning), I recommend keeping the following items with you:

- A highlighter – To mark important lines, quotes, or concepts.
- A black refill pen – For writing notes, underlining key points, or adding your own thoughts.
- Post-it-notes or sticky notes – To bookmark important pages or add reminders.

2. How to Read Effectively

Reading isn't just about going through the words—it's about understanding, remembering, and applying what you read. Here are some simple techniques to make your reading more effective:

•   Highlight Key Points – Whenever you come across a quote, sentence, or idea that feels important, immediately highlight it so you can find it easily later.

•   Mark Important Pages – If you find a page that contains crucial information, use a sticky note to bookmark it so you can quickly return to it.

•   Take Notes in the Margins – If you have thoughts, questions, or insights while reading, write them in the margins of the book. This helps reinforce learning and makes it easier to review later.

•   Read What's Relevant – You don't always have to read an entire book in order. If a specific chapter or section is relevant to you, focus on that first.

Sharvesh Sivakumar

PART-1
LIFE

WAKING UP EARLY

Many of us often say we don't have time, but let's be honest, that's often not the full truth. If we're truly being honest with ourselves, it's more about how we're spending our time. One simple thing that can do to significantly improve your day is waking up early. When you start your day earlier, you essentially get more time in a day -your day feels longer and more fulfilling. I understand that it is hard, it was hard when I started but eventually I started feeling weird when I sleep past of my daily wake up time.

For me, there are two major advantages I've noticed since making the decision to wake up early:

Increased Energy:

When you wake up earlier, you give yourself a head start. You can have that quiet, peaceful time where you're not rushing around. Your mind is still fresh from the night's rest, and you have more time to energize yourself through activities that will prepare you for a productive day. Maybe it's a workout, a healthy breakfast, or just enjoying the stillness of the morning. Regardless, it leads to a boost in energy that carries you through the day.

Better Sleep Quality:
 Though it may seem counterintuitive at first, waking up early can actually improve the quality of your sleep. When you wake up at the same time every day, your body starts to develop a routine, and this consistency improves your natural sleep cycle. You'll find that you fall asleep faster and sleep more soundly, which means you're truly recharging your body overnight.

If you're aiming for productivity, waking up early can be a game-changer. The key challenge for many of us is that we often use our phones as soon as we wake up. This is a productivity killer. Scrolling through social media or checking messages as soon as you wake up can easily waste a good chunk of time that you could've spent more productively. If you commit to waking up early, you'll realize that there's a whole extra window of time before the world starts demanding your attention. You can use this time for personal growth, creativity, or simply getting ahead with tasks before the usual distractions.

Another benefit of waking up early is that it positively impacts your mental health. The calmness in the early morning allow you to focus inward. You might feel like there are things you want to do or explore but feel self-conscious doing them around others-whether it's journaling, doing a quick workout, or you can just put some music and vibe with it. These activities can help to clear your mind, reduce stress, and give you a sense of accomplishment before the world even gets going. It's a time for *you*, where you can prioritize your personal growth without any external judgment.

However, it's important to acknowledge that this change won't feel easy at first, it is going to be hard. When I started waking up early, I initially felt tired and sluggish. My body wasn't used to the shift, and it took some time for my system to adjust. But it's vital to push through that initial phase. Once you get past it, you'll begin to notice how much more energized and focused you feel as the days go by. Eventually, waking up early won't just become a habit-it will become something that motivates you to make the most of every day. If you are not doing it already then atleast do it right next day, trust me it works. Waking up early is not the best thing that you can do, it is the must thing that you must do.

Since waking up early is difficult, here's my best trick that I used to wake up at 5 am instead of 7. Get your phone or alarm clock (alarm clock is the best),set an alarm 1 minute early than usual, for example if your daily time is 7 then set the alarm at 6:59. Do this daily so that by a month you would be waking up 30 minutes early.

EXERCISE

Waking up early and exercising can greatly enhance both your physical and mental well-being. Here's why:

1. Improved Focus

Exercise primes your brain, releasing chemicals like dopamine and serotonin that boost mood and cognitive function. Waking up early and working out helps improve focus and productivity throughout the day. Skipping exercise is like going to a movie and falling asleep—you miss out on the benefits of being alert and present.

2. Consistency Is Key

Exercise might be tough at first, but consistency is essential. Start small—20-minute sessions are enough to see results. The key is making it a habit, and over time, it becomes easier and more rewarding.

3. Boosts Confidence

Exercise not only shapes your body but also builds self-esteem. Regular workouts make you feel stronger and more in control, leading to increased confidence. Even if muscle growth is slow at first, the foundation you build now will pay off later.

4. Better Sleep

Physical activity helps your body rest better at night. When you exercise, your body craves rest and recovery, leading to improved sleep quality and a more refreshed morning.

5. Social Motivation

If exercising feels tough, find a workout buddy. Exercising with someone can make it more fun and keep you accountable, turning workouts into friendly competition and boosting motivation.

Quote by Sahil Bloom:

"There is no such thing as a loser who wakes up at 5 AM and works out."

This mindset underscores the discipline and growth that comes from consistently waking up early and committing to a workout routine.

My Experience:

Since I started working out, I've noticed several advantages:

Better Focus: Exercise helps me concentrate better on tasks.

Increased Stamina: I feel more energetic throughout the day.

Boosted Confidence: Regular exercise has increased my self-esteem and body confidence.

Ultimately, exercise not only improves your body but also helps with focus, sleep, and mental well-being. After all this the important, key point is you would look better. If you haven't started yet, give it a try. Trust me, it works. If you want a plan then use this:

Day 1- Arm
Day 2- Leg
Day 3- Abs
Day 4- Rest
Day 5- Shoulder
Day 6- Rest
Day 7- Abs

Understanding Emotions and Mood Swings

Why Do You Feel This Way?

As you grow older, you might notice changes in the way you feel and think. You may enjoy spending more time with friends at school rather than at home with your family. This is because, at this stage, friendships become an essential part of your life. You connect more easily with people your age, who understand your interests, experiences, and struggles.

At the same time, you may start feeling like your parents don't understand you as well as they used to. They might set rules that you find unfair or fail to see things from your perspective. This can be frustrating, but it's important to remember that this feeling is normal. All that stuff is not bad until it hurts someone. Always remember to go to your parents and just talk—shouting won't solve the problem. Most people your age experience this as they start gaining more independence. Your parents still care about you, even if they don't always express it in a way you understand. Instead of shutting them out, try to talk to them about your feelings. Clear communication can help them see things from your point of view and make your relationship better.

Why Do Moods Change So Quickly?

Have you ever felt extremely happy one moment, only to suddenly feel angry or sad the next? You might get excited about something small, then feel irritated for no clear reason. This rapid change in emotions can be confusing, but it's completely normal. And even your friends have same thing going so understand them.

At this stage of life, your body is going through many physical and hormonal changes. These changes can affect your emotions, making you feel overwhelmed, sensitive, or even moody at times. One moment, you may feel confident and energetic, and the next, you may feel frustrated or upset over small things. These emotional ups and downs are a natural part of growing up, and you're not alone in experiencing them.

While mood swings can sometimes feel frustrating, understanding why they happen can help you manage them better. The good news is that as you grow older, you'll learn how to control your emotions more effectively.

How to Manage Mood Swings and Emotions

Even though mood swings are normal, learning how to handle them in a healthy way can make life much easier. Here are some ways to manage your emotions:

1. Identify Your Triggers

Pay attention to what makes you feel happy, angry, or sad. Is it a particular situation, a conversation, or even a certain thought? Understanding where is the trigger of the gun you are holding.

2. Take a Deep Breath Before Reacting

When you feel overwhelmed by emotions, take a moment to pause. Breathe deeply, count to ten, or step away from the situation before reacting.

This simple technique can help you avoid saying or doing something you might regret later.

3. Express Your Feelings in a Healthy Way

Bottling up emotions can make them feel even stronger. Instead of keeping everything inside, try to express how you feel. You can talk to a trusted friend, family member, or even write in a journal. Sometimes, just putting your feelings into words can help you understand them better.

4. Take Care of Your Body

Believe it or not, your physical health plays a big role in your emotions. If you don't get enough sleep, eat unhealthy foods, or avoid exercise, your mood may become more unstable. Make sure you:

Get at least 7-9 hours of sleep every night.

Eat nutritious meals with plenty of fruits and vegetables.

Engage in physical activities like walking, playing sports, or dancing.

Taking care of your body can help balance your emotions and improve your overall well-being.

5. Do Things That Make You Feel Good

When you're feeling low, try doing something that brings you joy. Listen to music, draw, play a sport, read a book, or spend time with people who make you happy. Engaging in activities you love can help lift your mood and make difficult moments easier to handle.

6. Accept that it's Okay to Feel Emotional

Some days, you might feel more sensitive than usual, and that's completely fine. Emotions are a natural part of life, and everyone experiences ups and downs. Instead of feeling bad about your emotions, accept them.

Persistence

Why Consistency Beats Intensity

We all dream of success—better grades, a fitter body, a stronger mind, or a happier life. And when we get excited about change, we often go all in. We push ourselves hard. We try to do everything at once.

But here's the truth most people ignore:

Success doesn't come from one big push. It comes from small actions, done every day.

Consistency beats intensity.

What Most People Get Wrong

A lot of people start with passion and energy. They:

Go to the gym for two hours on Day 1, then quit by Day 5.

Study all night for an exam, but forget it all a week later.

Try waking up at 5 AM and give up because they feel tired and frustrated.

This is the mistake: relying on intensity-short, extreme effort.

It feels powerful in the moment, but it doesn't last.

Real success comes from small, steady actions done again and again.

Why Consistency Is Powerful

Imagine this:

Reading 10 pages a day = around 3,600 pages a year = 12 books.

Exercising 15 minutes a day = over 90 hours of movement a year.

Writing 200 words a day = a full novel in a year.

None of these things sound hard. But doing them every day? That's where the real challenge—and the real power—is.

Consistency builds discipline. Consistency creates momentum. Consistency leads to mastery.

How Consistency Creates Long-Term Results

Here's how it works in different areas of life:

☐ Learning – Studying daily helps your brain retain information. It's like watering a plant: regular drops matter more than dumping a bucket once.

☐ Fitness – Gradual effort helps your body grow stronger without injury or burnout. It's better to do 10 push-ups a day than 100 once a month.

☐ Personal Growth – Journaling or reflecting for a few minutes a day builds emotional intelligence and self-awareness.

☐ Goals – When you take one step every day, you make more progress in a month than with a giant leap that leads to exhaustion.

Small habits add up. They build character. They build confidence.

How to Stay Consistent (Even When You Don't Feel Like It)

1. Start Small

Don't aim for perfection. Start with what feels too easy. If it's too hard, you won't stick with it.

2. Make It Daily

Even if it's just 2 minutes, doing it daily creates rhythm and routine.

3. Track Progress

Use a notebook, app, or calendar. Seeing your streak builds motivation.

4. Have Clear Goals

Instead of "get better at reading," say "read 5 pages every night before bed."

5. Don't Chase Motivation

Motivation comes and goes. Discipline is stronger. Set a time and stick to it.

6. Be Kind to Yourself

Missed a day? That's okay. One bad day doesn't break the habit—quitting does. Just restart.

7. Build Systems, Not Pressure

Create an environment that supports your habit. Keep your book near your bed. Lay out your workout clothes the night before.

JOURNAL

Journaling has become a game-changer for many people, and when they say, "This is the one thing that changed my life," they're speaking from experience. It's not just a trendy activity—it's something that can really transform your life, especially when you use it with intention. For me, as a teenager, I wanted a way to record my thoughts, track my progress, and document my journey. That's when I stumbled upon journaling through YouTube, and once I tried it, I quickly realized just how beneficial it was.

The Power of a Journal: A Life Archive

The idea of journaling goes beyond just writing down events; it's about capturing your life's essence in a single book. I created my own journal layout, which I refer to as a "life archive." It's not just a place to jot down what I did every day—it's a record of my growth, thoughts, goals, and dreams. This notebook has become a personal timeline, a place where I can see how far I've come and how I've evolved. Whenever I need a snapshot of a specific day, I simply flip back to my journal. It's like having a personal archive of my entire life, all in one place.

Clarity of Thought

One of the best benefits of journaling is the clarity it provides. Sometimes, our minds get overwhelmed with endless thoughts, and it's hard to focus or even understand what we're feeling. Writing down your thoughts helps you sort through that mental clutter and brings a sense of order. When you see your thoughts on paper, they become clearer and easier to analyze. Journaling also helps you process emotions and ideas that might otherwise remain tangled up in your mind.

Increased Productivity

Journaling also boosts productivity by helping you organize your goals. When you write things down, you get a clear view of what you want to achieve and how to break it into smaller, actionable steps. I've found that setting daily or weekly goals in my journal has made me more accountable to myself. It's easy to get lost in day-to-day distractions, but when you have a visual reminder of your goals; it becomes much easier to stay focused and productive. It also helps you reflect on what's working and what isn't, allowing you to adjust your strategy as needed.

A Record of Your Journey

Perhaps the most significant benefit of journaling is how it helps you remember and reflect on your past. Have you ever wished you could remember exactly what you did on a certain day or how you felt during a particular event? With journaling, you can. Your journal acts as a personal archive that records your thoughts, actions, and experiences. Whether it's something as simple as a funny memory or a breakthrough moment, your journal can help you look back on your life and see how much you've grown over time.

Create Your Own Layout

The beauty of journaling is that it's highly customizable. There is no real method of journaling, I designed my own layout to suit my needs, and I've found that it really helps me in many ways. My layout includes spaces for tracking my goals, jotting down daily reflections, and even recording things I'm grateful for. It gives me structure and direction, which is why I've made it such a regular part of my life. However, I encourage you to create your own layout. The best journal for you is the one that serves your personal needs and lifestyle. Experiment with different formats, components, and sections until you find what works for you. But if you're not sure where to start, feel free to use my layout—it's designed with intention and has benefited me in countless ways.

The Power of Journaling: A Quote to Remember

David Allen, a productivity expert, once said:

"Your mind is for having ideas, not for holding them."

This quote perfectly sums up why journaling is so important. Our brains are meant to generate ideas, not hold onto every little detail. By putting your thoughts, ideas, and plans into a journal, you free up mental space for creativity and focus. You no longer have to keep everything in your head, which reduces stress and makes room for new ideas. You can actually write anything in that note or diary, there is no limit.

Trust me when I say journaling works. It's not just a task to cross off your to-do list—it's an investment in you. Make it as a day to day habit that you will do no matter what. It will help you track your progress, gain clarity, increase your productivity, and provide a meaningful record of your life. As you create your own journal layout, remember that there are no right or wrong ways to do it. The goal is to find something that suits your needs and helps you stay focused, organized, and reflective. So, start journaling today—it's a simple habit that can make a huge difference in your life

PART-2

PRODUCTIVITY

Procrastination

The Enemy of Success

Procrastination is not just a bad habit—it's one of the biggest threats to your growth, goals, and future success. The more you procrastinate, the further you drift from your dreams. It's like running a race but constantly stopping to tie your shoelaces -again and again-until you're left behind.

So what exactly is procrastination?

It's the act of delaying or postponing important tasks. At first, it feels harmless—maybe even fun. But over time, it leads to stress, missed deadlines, wasted potential, and frustration. You might feel like you're relaxing in the moment, but in reality, you're setting yourself up for panic later.

As Abraham Lincoln once said:

> *"You cannot escape the responsibility of tomorrow by evading it today."*

This quote says it all. You can't outrun the work you delay. It eventually catches up with you—stronger and heavier than before.

The Cycle of Procrastination

Let's look at a typical student's school year.

First month: You have a few assignments, maybe some light reading. Nothing major. You tell yourself, "I'll do it tomorrow."

Mid-year: Deadlines are stacking up. Your planner is full, but your completed tasks? Not so much. Now you're overwhelmed.

End of year: The panic kicks in. Exams are coming. Projects are due. But you're not prepared. And suddenly, it feels like there's no way to catch up.

This is the cycle of procrastination. It starts small but grows quickly. The earlier you break it, the better.

FDEs: Focus-Destroying Experts

One of the biggest causes of procrastination today is the smartphone. More specifically—FDEs (Focus-Destroying Experts). These are apps or digital habits that steal your attention and offer nothing useful in return.

Examples of FDEs:

Endless scrolling on social media: Instagram, TikTok, or YouTube Shorts can trap you for hours.

Watching random videos: "Just one more video" turns into ten.

Playing addictive games: They feel rewarding but waste precious time.

Checking notifications constantly: Every buzz distracts you and breaks your focus.

These apps are designed to be addictive. They're not your friends they're thieves of your time.

How to Overcome Procrastination

1. Eliminate Distractions

Start by cleaning your digital environment. Delete FDE apps. Turn off non-essential notifications. Create a phone usage limit. Remember your phone is a tool, not a toy.

> Tip: Keep your phone in another room while studying.

2. Follow the Two-Minute Rule

If something takes less than two minutes just do it now. Reply to that message. File that paper. Hang your bag. These small wins prevent a mountain of tiny tasks from building up later.

3. Break Big Tasks into Small Steps

Big tasks like exam revision or writing a project can feel impossible. But when you break them down page by page, or step by step they become manageable.

> Example: "Study science" becomes → Read 2 pages of the textbook + take notes.

4. Set Deadlines and Stick to Them

Without deadlines, you keep postponing. So create personal deadlines even for small things. Use a calendar or planner to track them. And here's the key: treat your self-made deadlines seriously.

5. Use the 5-Second Rule

Whenever you catch yourself thinking, "I'll do it later," count down from 5 to 1 and take action before your brain talks you out of it. It works because it interrupts the delay pattern.

> "5… 4… 3… 2… 1… GO!"

This small trick beats overthinking.

6. Reward Yourself

Make work feel rewarding. After completing a study session or finishing homework, reward yourself with something small—like 10 minutes of a show, a snack, or a short walk. This turns work into a challenge with a prize.

News letters

A Powerful Resource for Gaining Knowledge

In today's fast-paced world, staying informed isn't just an option—it's a necessity. Whether you want to learn about personal growth, current trends, science, or new technology, there's one underrated tool that can make a huge difference: newsletters. These short, information-packed emails deliver valuable insights directly to your inbox, often weekly or even daily.

Why Newsletters Are a Great Learning Tool

Unlike books, which demand dedicated time and energy, newsletters are designed for quick learning. You can read one in just 2–5 minutes. Imagine making real progress in your knowledge just by checking your inbox during a break, while commuting, or right after waking up. These small reading sessions might not seem like much, but over time, they can lead to huge improvements in your awareness, mindset, and even career skills.

> ☐ Example: Let's say you subscribe to a weekly newsletter about psychology. Each issue explains one useful mental model or mindset shift. In a year, you'll have 52 solid tools to use in daily life- without reading a single 300-page book.

The Benefits of Reading Newsletters

1. ☐ Time-Efficient Learning

Most newsletters are short and straight to the point. You don't need an hour-just a few minutes can give you something new to think about.

2. ☐ Regular Updates

Books take years to write and publish, but newsletters give you fresh information every week. Whether it's the latest research, trends, or lessons from experts, you'll stay current without feeling overwhelmed.

3. ☐ Wide Range of Topics

There's a newsletter for everything: mindset, productivity, health, career, finance, science, education, and more. You can explore many interests without having to buy dozens of books.

4. ☐ Cost-Effective (Often Free)

The best part? Most newsletters are completely free. Some even offer premium versions, but the free editions already give tons of value.

5. ☐ Easy to Consume Anywhere

Whether you're on your phone, tablet, or laptop, newsletters are mobile-friendly and convenient. You can learn something valuable during a school break or before bed.

6. ☐ Discovery and Curiosity

Newsletters often link to new ideas, tools, apps, or books you've never heard of. It's like having a smart friend who shares what's interesting every week.

How to Get the Most Out of Newsletters

Don't Subscribe to Too Many: Choose 3–5 high-quality newsletters that match your interests. Too many will clutter your inbox and reduce focus.

Read with a Purpose: Highlight or jot down key ideas that inspire you.

Unsubscribe Without Guilt: If a newsletter no longer helps you, just unsubscribe. Focus only on what adds value.

Set a Time: Choose a time to check newsletters weekly, like Sunday mornings or after school. Make it a habit.

You Can Even Write Your Own Newsletter

Once you learn something valuable, why not share it? Writing a newsletter helps you:

Teach what you learn

Build a personal brand

Improve your writing skills

Earn money (some writers make full-time income from newsletters through sponsorships and paid versions)

> ✍🗆 Example: A teenager passionate about productivity could start a weekly newsletter called "Better Every Week," where they share a tip, book summary, or personal experience. Over time, this can grow into a community.

My Experience With Newsletters

Personally, I don't write a newsletter (yet!), but I read several. They help me stay informed, think more clearly, and explore different fields without getting bored. I've learned about writing, self-discipline, entrepreneurship, and even fitness—all from newsletters.

Sharvesh Sivakumar

The Pomodoro Technique
A Smarter Way to Study

Have you ever felt tired after long study sessions—even though you didn't get much done? You're not alone. Many students think that studying for hours is the key to success, but our brains don't work that way. What we really need is a better way to manage our time and energy.

That's where the Pomodoro Technique comes in.

What is the Pomodoro Technique?

The Pomodoro Technique is a time management method that helps you stay focused and avoid burnout. It works by breaking your work into short, intense periods of concentration followed by short breaks.

Here's how it works:

1. Pick a Task – Choose what you want to work on.

2. Set a Timer – Work for 25 minutes without distractions.

3. Take a Break – Rest for 5 minutes.

4. Repeat – After four sessions, take a longer break (15–30 minutes).

This method trains your brain to focus and recharge at the right times.

Why It Works So Well

☐ Improves Focus – Short work sessions keep your attention sharp.

☐ Prevents Burnout – Regular breaks help you stay energized.

☐ Reduces Procrastination – "Just 25 minutes" feels easy to start.

☐ Increases Productivity – You get more done with less stress.

Sharvesh Sivakumar

My Experience: How It Helped Us Study Better

My friend Bhavin and I used to study for hours and still feel tired and unproductive. Then we tried the Pomodoro Technique.

We set a 25-minute timer, focused fully, then took 5-minute breaks. After four rounds, we took a longer break. It felt surprisingly easy and effective.

We remembered more

We didn't feel exhausted

Studying became enjoyable

We weren't working harder—we were working smarter.

Tips for Using the Pomodoro Technique Effectively

☐ Avoid Distractions – Silence your phone and find a quiet space.

☐ Use a Timer – Apps like Pomofocus or TomatoTimer help.

☐ Adjust If Needed – Try 50/10 sessions if 25/5 feels too short.

☐ Take Good Breaks – Stretch, walk, or drink water—don't scroll!

How to Read 30 Books per Year Even When You Go to School

A Realistic Guide for Students to Build a Daily Reading Habit

Many YouTubers and self-help authors often say, "You should read more!" But they rarely explain how to actually do it—especially if you're a student juggling school, homework, exams, friends, and maybe even a few hobbies. That's why this guide is not just motivational—it's practical.

Let's dive into a student-friendly system that makes consistent reading a daily habit, not a random activity.

1. The Mindset: Why Students Should Read

Reading isn't just for toppers or nerds. It's one of the most powerful habits any teenager can build. Here's why:

Improves vocabulary and communication – useful in school exams, debates, and even interviews.

Builds concentration – a superpower in the age of distractions.

Develops imagination and empathy -- helping you understand people and life better.

Sharpens your brain – reading is a workout for your mind.

When you think of reading as mental growth, not just a school task, you'll feel more

excited about it.

2. Buy Books in Bulk: Stock Before You Start

One of the biggest mistakes beginners make? They read one book, finish it, and then wait weeks before getting the next. This kills momentum.

Tip: Always have the next book ready.

If you have ☐ 2000 to invest in books, you can buy around 6–7 books (depending on the price). Buying in bulk helps in 3 ways:

Saves time – no waiting between books.

Saves money – discounts on bundles or offers.

Builds urgency – seeing a pile of unread books motivates you to read.

Bonus tip: If you're on a tight budget, borrow from a library, exchange with friends, or read free e-books (many classics are available online).

3. The Math of Reading (How Much Should You Read?)

Let's break it down step-by-step, using simple math that fits a student's daily schedule.

Average reading speed: 300 words per minute

Approximate reading speed: 50 pages per hour

Even if you're slower than that, it's okay. Let's keep 1 hour of reading = 40–50 pages

Now let's calculate the yearly reading potential:

Daily → 50 pages × 1 hour

Weekly → 50 pages × 7 = 350 pages = 1 book (on average)

Monthly → 1 book × 4 = 4 books

Yearly → 4 × 12 = 48 books per year

But let's be honest—school life is unpredictable.

4. Adjust for Real Life (Festivals, Exams, Burnout)

You're not a robot. Sometimes you won't be able to read:

Festivals

Family trips

Illness

Sports days or school events

Exams and revision periods

That's why we subtract 18 books from the ideal yearly plan.

10 books for breaks, holidays, or tired days

8 books for exam preparation time

☐ Final Reading Goal: 48 - 18 = 30 Books Per Year

That's still an amazing number. Even if you miss a few more days, you'll still be ahead of 99% of people your age.

5. Practical Strategies to Make Reading a Daily Habit

Here's where most people fail. They don't build a reading system.

☐ Make Reading a Part of Your Daily Routine

Read before bed (instead of phone scrolling)

Read while commuting (bus, train, or waiting in line)

Read during school breaks or lunch

Read in the morning after waking up

☐ Carry a Book Everywhere

A physical book in your bag

An e-book on your phone or Kindle app

Audiobooks (great for multitasking like walking)

☐ Set a Daily Time Goal

If 1 hour is hard, start with just 15–30 minutes daily

Use a timer (like Pomodoro: 25 mins reading, 5 mins break)

☐ Use a Reading Tracker

Mark how many pages/chapters you read daily

Keep a reading journal or app like Goodreads

6. Use School Holidays Smartly

Holidays = your reading booster.

Summer Vacation (4–6 weeks): You can finish 6–8 books easily if you read 1 hour/day

Winter Holidays or weekends: Great time for catching up or starting a new book

Plan a holiday reading challenge: "5 books in 30 days" or "100 pages per day for 2 weeks"

The Habit of Writing a Book:
A Powerful Way to Learn and Grow

In a world filled with distractions and quick entertainment, writing a book might seem like an old-fashioned or impossible task—especially for young people. But the truth is, writing a book is one of the most powerful habits you can build as a teenager or student. Not only does it improve your academic and communication skills, but it also transforms the way you think, grow, and express yourself.

Why Writing a Book Changes You

When I began writing my first book, I thought it would be a simple way to share my thoughts. But soon I discovered that the process of writing wasn't just about putting words on a page—it was about challenging myself to grow. Writing forces you to slow down and think. It demands clarity, research, planning, and creativity.

Unlike reading, which gives you information, writing makes you interact with that information. You question it, break it down, rebuild it in your own words, and make it understandable for others. This changes how deeply you understand a topic. In fact, writing a book is like teaching—and teaching is one of the best ways to learn.

Benefits of Writing a Book

1. Deep Learning and Mastery

Writing a book makes you understand your subject far more deeply than surface-level reading. You have to explain things clearly, which means you must understand them well yourself. Every sentence you write reflects your clarity—or confusion. This pushes you to study better and ask better questions.

2. Improved Research Skills

To create meaningful content, you'll find yourself reading books, watching documentaries, studying articles, and even talking to experts. This strengthens your ability to find and judge good information—an important skill in school and life.

3. Creative Expression

Writing helps you discover your voice. Your opinions, experiences, metaphors, and examples are yours alone. A book gives you the power to express these in your own style. This is not just fun—it's freeing. It helps you think for yourself in a world full of copied opinions.

4. Earning Potential

While writing should be driven by passion, it's also true that books can be sold. Even a short ebook can earn money if written with effort and marketed well. You can use this income to support your studies, buy better tools, or save for future goals.

5. Confidence and Personal Growth

Completing a book is no small task. It takes weeks, sometimes months. But once you finish, you realize something amazing—you actually did it. This builds mental toughness and self-belief. You'll feel ready to take on other challenges too.

Making Your Book a Success

Writing is one part. Sharing it with the world is another. Here's how to make your book reach the readers it deserves:

1. Give 100% Effort

Writing half-heartedly won't get you far. Your book should reflect your best thinking and deepest understanding. If you want readers to value your words, give them your best work.

2. Research Thoroughly

Make your book trustworthy by backing it up with solid facts, example.

PART-3
SCHOOL

Competition

A Strategy for Academic Success

If you want to achieve high marks and become a topper, one essential ingredient is competition. But not just any competition—the right kind. True academic success doesn't come from trying to defeat the best student overnight. It comes from smartly choosing your battles—finding someone slightly ahead of you and steadily rising.

Why the Right Competitor Matters

Think of competition like climbing stairs. If you try to jump to the top in one leap, you'll fall. But if you go one step at a time, you build momentum—and eventually, you reach the top.

Your competitor should be someone who challenges you but doesn't overwhelm you. A person just one or two steps ahead keeps you on your toes while still making the goal feel achievable.

Choosing the Right Competitor

If you're currently ranked 6th or 7th, don't stress about the 1st ranker just yet. Focus on students ranked 4th or 5th. Observe how they study, how they approach tests, and how they manage time. Once you've reached that level, aim for 3rd. And if you reach 2nd place? You know what to do— compete with the topper.

This step-by-step approach helps you build momentum, track progress, and stay consistently motivated.

Why This Method Works

1. Keeps You Motivated

Competing with someone just a little better than you gives you a sense of hope and energy. It's challenging but within reach—so you stay hungry for improvement.

2. Prevents Discouragement

Competing with someone miles ahead might feel like a never-ending race. This leads to burnout, frustration, and loss of interest. Smart competition avoids this trap.

3. Ensures Continuous Progress

As you move up the ranks, your targets change. Every time you reach a new level, there's a new benchmark—keeping your academic journey fresh and forward-moving.

4. Builds Real Confidence

Success builds confidence. Beating someone close to your level shows that your effort is paying off—and that you're capable of even more.

Applying This Strategy Effectively

Here's how to make this strategy work in real life:

Observe Your Competitor

What are they doing differently? Are they using flashcards, practicing more problems, or waking up earlier? Pay attention—not to copy everything, but to learn smarter methods.

Adopt Their Best Practices

If a student ranks higher, it's not by luck. Maybe they revise daily, take self-tests, or ask teachers questions regularly. Try adopting at least one good habit from them.

Stay Consistent

One day of intense study won't help as much as small, regular efforts. Just like you don't grow tall in one day, academic growth takes time and steady progress.

Challenge Yourself

Get out of your comfort zone. Try solving tougher questions, studying for 15 extra minutes, or writing one more practice answer than usual. Growth happens at the edge of effort.

Friends: The Two Types of Friends You Need in Life

Friendship is one of the most beautiful and powerful parts of human life. It's not about how many people you know, but how deeply you're connected to a few. True friends are rare, and finding the right ones can make your life feel lighter, stronger, and more meaningful. But not all friends serve the same role in your life.

Over time, I realized something important:
We all need two types of friends in life—

1. Friends who need you, and

2. Friends whom you need

These categories may seem simple, but understanding the difference between them can change the way you view your relationships forever.

1. Friends Who Need You

These are the friends who see you as an important part of their life. They lean on you. They open up to you. They trust you with their feelings, their stories, and their struggles. You are not just a person to them—you are a support system.

Why They Matter

When someone needs you, it means you matter to them. They care about what you say, how you feel, and where your friendship is going. Their loyalty is strong, not because you're perfect, but because you are irreplaceable to them.

How to Identify These Friends

•	They check in on you regularly, not just when they want something.

•	They stick by you even when you're not doing well.

• They celebrate your small wins and never feel jealous.

• They stand up for you when you're not around.

• They forgive easily, because they care more about keeping the bond than keeping score.

These friends give your life stability. When the world feels unpredictable, their presence gives you a sense of security and emotional grounding.

> ☐ Life tip: Never take these friends for granted. If someone needs you and values you, it's a sign that you bring light into their life.

2. Friends Whom You Need

This group is different. These are the friends you look up to. They may inspire you, guide you, or challenge you to become better. You feel stronger, smarter, or more motivated when you're around them. Maybe they're wiser, more confident, or just have a vibe that lifts you up.

Why They Matter

These friends bring value to your personal growth. They don't just support you emotionally—they help shape your thinking, influence your habits, or open new doors for you. Sometimes, you need someone to look up to, someone who shows you what's possible.

How to Identify These Friends

They have a strength or quality you admire—like kindness, leadership, honesty, or wisdom.

You often learn something from them, even if it's unspoken.
They motivate you to improve, work harder, or be more disciplined.
They may not need you back, but they respect you and help when they can.

These friendships can feel unbalanced at times, because you might need them more than they need you. But that's okay—as long as you're aware of that dynamic and don't rely too heavily on it emotionally.

> ☐ Life tip: Be careful not to confuse admiration with friendship. Sometimes we chase people because they inspire us, but they may not be invested in us the same way. Learn from them, but don't lose yourself.

3. The Ideal Friend: A Balance of Both

The rarest and most beautiful kind of friend is someone who both needs you and whom you also need. This is the friendship that feels equal, honest, and whole. Neither side is giving too much or too little. It's a partnership.

What Makes This Friendship Special

- Mutual trust – You both feel safe opening up without judgment.

- Emotional support – You're both there for each other in tough times.

- Shared growth – You challenge and inspire one another to improve.

- No fear of losing – Because the bond is strong and based on mutual respect.

- Loyalty through time – Even when life changes, the connection stays.

These are the friendships that can last a lifetime. They grow deeper over the years because both people are willing to invest effort, patience, and love into them.

USE YOUR SPARE TIME

As a school student, we often overlook the amount of free time we have throughout the day. We tend to get caught up in chatting with friends, scrolling on our phones, or just wandering around the classroom, but if we pay attention, we can find pockets of time that can be used more productively. Let me give you a few examples. I am usually popular for completing my homework in school, and even this book I wrote 90% of it in the school.

Making the Most of School Time

For instance, after finishing your lunch, many of us end up chatting with friends or just hanging out (roaming around the campus). Instead of that, consider using that time to complete the easiest homework or assignments while you're still at school. It's something I did in the past, especially during my 6th and 7th grades. As I mentioned before I became well known for completing my math homework during math class, while the teacher would be giving notes or explaining new exercises. I'd finish the whole assignment during class, and then during the lunch break, I'd work on other homework that didn't need immediate attention.

By completing homework during school hours, I would leave more free time at home to focus on tougher assignments that required more concentration. This way, I was able to manage my workload more effectively and reduce the amount of stress after school.

Utilizing Free Time for Personal Growth

Now, think about the free time you have after finishing your homework. Instead of mindlessly scrolling through social media or binge-watching videos, you could use that time to invest in something meaningful. For example, you could pick up a book and read a story that interests you, or better yet, learn something new every day. I started learning Python in my free time, and it was one of the best decisions I made. It might seem challenging at first, but with a little consistency, it becomes more enjoyable and rewarding.

The time we think we don't have can easily be turned into valuable opportunities for personal growth, whether it's reading, learning a new skill, or improving existing ones.

YouTube Channels for Learning

One of the best ways to make use of free time is by consuming educational content. There are many YouTube channels that helped me grow and improve in various areas of life.. Whether you want to learn programming, improve your study habits, or just get inspired, there's a wealth of content out there to help you on your journey.

The bottom line is, we often have more time than we realize. By shifting how we use it, we can achieve so much more. Instead of wasting it, we can develop new skills, improve ourselves, and stay ahead. So, next time you find yourself with free time, think about how you could use it to better your future. Whether it's reading, learning, or even finishing homework ahead of time, it all adds up to a productive and fulfilling day.

The Power of Group Studying

Many people believe that studying should be an individual effort, where one sits alone with books and focuses on learning. However, research has shown that students tend to achieve higher marks when they study in groups. Group study not only helps in better understanding but also promotes collaboration, active learning, and improved retention of information.

However, for a study group to be effective, it is crucial to select the right members. A well-balanced study group should ideally consist of four types of learners, each playing a unique role in the learning process. These members complement each other's strengths and weaknesses, making the group dynamic and productive.

The Four Key Members of a Study Group

1. The Topper (Mentor & Guide)
- This student is the most knowledgeable in the group.

•   They have a deep understanding of the subjects and concepts.

•   Their role is to teach others in the group, helping them grasp difficult topics.

•   This student is the must in every group

They provide clarity and structured explanations, ensuring that every member understands the material.

2. The Average Student (The Bridge Between Learners)

•   This student is neither the best nor the weakest but falls in between.

•   They learn from the topper and then help explain concepts in simpler terms to those who struggle.

•   They act as a bridge between the advanced and weaker students, reinforcing their own understanding in the process.

•   By adding them to group they eventually turn into topper.

3. The Second Topper (The Problem Solver)

•	This student is also academically strong but focuses more on clearing doubts.

•	They help clarify any confusion and ensure that everyone in the group fully understands the material.

•	Their role is to reinforce concepts and offer alternative explanations if needed.

4. The Slow Learner (The Learner & Absorber)

•	This student may struggle with understanding concepts quickly.

•	Their primary role is to learn from the others and absorb knowledge at their own pace.

•	With the support of the group, they gain confidence and improve over time.

•	They first turn into an average learner and also a topper in the future.

Their presence is essential, as teaching weaker students helps others strengthen their understanding.

Why This Study Method Works?

Active Engagement: Group study encourages students to engage actively in discussions rather than passively reading textbooks.

Better Retention: Explaining concepts to others helps reinforce one's own understanding, making the knowledge stick.

Collaboration & Support: Students can motivate and support each other, reducing stress and making learning more enjoyable.

Clarification of Doubts: Weak areas are addressed more effectively as doubts are cleared through peer discussions.

Time Management: Studying in a group promotes discipline and better time management, ensuring efficient use of study hours. If done correctly, group studying can be a powerful tool for academic success. A well-structured group with the right mix of members ensures that everyone benefits. So, if you want to improve your grades and make learning more effective, try studying in a group—it really works, trust me!

MY EXAM STUDY TECHNIQUE

A Practical Approach to Consistent and Smart Learning

I'm not a topper—not the #1 rank in the class. But I'm not at the bottom either. I float somewhere between the above-average group and the toppers. And that's okay. Because what matters more than rank is progress. Over time, I've crafted a study technique that helped me improve my marks, stay consistent, and reduce stress. It's not about studying for 6 hours straight or memorizing everything overnight. It's about studying smart, not just hard.

Let me share what worked for me—and might work for you too.

1. Build a Structured Daily Routine

People often talk about the power of waking up early—and I totally agree. But waking up early is useless if you don't use that time wisely. If you've read my earlier chapters about waking up early, exercising, and journaling, you already have a strong head start. These morning habits aren't random—they prepare your body and mind for focus and discipline.

How I Use My Morning:

Instead of jumping into textbook studying, I use the fresh, quiet morning hours for homework, assignments, and any pending tasks.

This clears my mind and frees up my evening for deep learning and revision.

Result? I end the day with meaningful study time without feeling stressed or rushed.

2. Use the Pomodoro Technique to Boost Focus

One of the most helpful techniques I've ever tried is the Pomodoro Technique. It sounds fancy, but it's super simple.

Here's how it works:
Study for 25 minutes with full focus.
Take a 5-minute break—stand up, stretch, drink water.

Repeat this 4 times.

After 4 sessions, take a longer break of 15–30 minutes.

This method works wonders because:

It trains your brain to focus for short bursts.

3. Adapt and Create Your Own System

Now, I'm not saying you have to copy everything I do. What works for me might not fit you perfectly. And that's the point.
The best study technique is not about doing what everyone else does. It's about understanding yourself:
Do you study better in the morning or evening?
Do you need music or silence?
Do you remember more by reading or writing?

Experiment. Try new techniques. Keep what works. Let go of what doesn't.
Your system doesn't have to be perfect—just effective.

ACTION PLAN

This segment is to male you get full content out of the book. The reason why I named it as action plan is cause in this segment you are going to take action for each one of the chapters that is you are going to take an initiative to take a step to improve your life by reading this. Let me explain the concept. If you go the next page there you will see a table, check the first column that is the chapter number and in the next one write the action that you are going to take for that respective that chapter. Date is for the date of when you are starting that action. Completion is to mean, after 30 you have to write the date of the particular day. That's it I think this might help you to change you routine.

Chap. No	Action that implement from the chapter	date	Comp
1			
2			
3			
4			
5			
6			
7			
8			
9			
10			
11			
12			
13			
14			
15